WHAT A WONDERFUL BIRD
THE FROG ARE

WHAT A WONDERFUL BIRD THE FROG ARE

An Assortment of Humorous
Poetry and Verse

Edited by
MYRA COHN LIVINGSTON

Harcourt Brace Jovanovich, Inc., New York

ISBN 0-15-295400-7
Library of Congress Catalog Card Number: 72-88171
Printed in the United States of America

Every effort has been made to trace the ownership of all copyrighted material
and to secure the necessary permissions to reprint these selections. In the event
of any question arising as to the use of any material, the editor and the publisher,
while expressing regret for any inadvertent error, will be happy to make the
necessary correction in future printings. Thanks are due to the following for permission to reprint the copyrighted material listed below:

GEORGE ALLEN & UNWIN LTD. for "The Great Auk's Ghost" from *The Last
Blackbird* by Ralph Hodgson.

APPLETON-CENTURY-CROFTS for "Bringing Him Up" by Lord Dunsany from
Number Four Joy Street.

ATHENEUM PUBLISHERS for "Historical Reflections" and "Wrath" by John Hol-
lander and "Higgledy-piggledy" by E. William Seaman from *Jiggery-Pokery*, A
Compendium of Double Dactyls edited by Anthony Hecht and John Hollander,
Copyright © 1966 by Anthony Hecht and John Hollander.

THE BOBBS-MERRILL COMPANY, INC., for "Better Come Quietly" from *New and
Selected Poems 1932–1967* by Peter Viereck, copyright © 1967, by Peter Viereck.

PETRA CABOT for "The Perfect Reactionary" by Hughes Mearns.

CHICAGO TRIBUNE for "The Dinosaur" by Bert Leston Taylor.

JOHN CIARDI for "After a Fire" and "To a Reviewer Who Admired My Book"
from *This Strangest Everything* by John Ciardi, c. 1966 by Rutgers, The State
University.

PEGGY BENNETT COLE for "Plain Talk for a Pachyderm."

COLLINS-KNOWLTON-WING, INC., for "Traveller's Curse After Misdirection"
from *Collected Poems, 1955* by Robert Graves, Copyright © 1955, by Robert
Graves.

CONSTABLE PUBLISHERS, LONDON, for "The Artist" and "The Wishes of an
Elderly Man" from *Laughter from a Cloud* by Sir Walter Raleigh; and for "Lao-
Tzŭ" by Po Chü-i and "On the Birth of His Son" by Su Tung-p'o from *170
Chinese Poems* translated by Arthur Waley.

HOUGHTON MIFFLIN COMPANY for "The Sycophantic Fox and the Gullible Raven" from *Grimm Tales Made Gay* by Guy Wetmore Carryl; and for "Mother Goose's Garland" from *Collected Poems 1917–1952* by Archibald MacLeish.

ALFRED A. KNOPF, INC., for "The Microbe" from *Cautionary Verses* by Hilaire Belloc, published 1941 by Alfred A. Knopf, Inc.; and for "Lao-Tzŭ" by Po Chü-i from "The Philosophers" and "On the Birth of His Son" by Su Tung-p'o, Copyright 1919, 1941 by Alfred A. Knopf, Inc., and Renewed 1947 by Arthur Waley, reprinted from *170 Chinese Poems,* translated by Arthur Waley.

MAXINE KUMIN for "The Microscope," Copyright © 1963, by The Atlantic Monthly Company, Boston, Mass.

J. B. LIPPINCOTT COMPANY for "Unearned Increment" from the book *Mandarin in Manhattan* by Christopher Morley, Copyright, 1933, by Christopher Morley, Renewal, ©, 1961 by Helen F. Morley.

LITTLE, BROWN AND COMPANY for "Gloss" from *Odds Without Ends* by David McCord, Copyright 1953, 1954 by David McCord; for "The Firefly" from *Good Intentions* by Ogden Nash, Copyright 1942, by Ogden Nash; and for "Kind of an Ode to Duty," "Parsley for Vice-President," and "The Purist" from *Verses from 1929 On* by Ogden Nash, Copyright, 1935 by The Curtis Publishing Company.

LIVERIGHT PUBLISHING CORPORATION, NEW YORK, for twenty-two lines from "Poems in Praise of Practically Nothing" and "Your Little Hands" from *A Treasury of Humorous Verse* by Samuel Hoffenstein, Copyright © 1946 by Liveright Publishing Corporation.

DAVID MC CORD for an excerpt from "Perambulator Poems," Copyright 1941 by David McCord, from *And What's More* published by Coward McCann; and for "Signs of the Zodiac."

THE MACMILLAN COMPANY for "Cynic's Epitaph" and "Inscription for a Peal of Eight Bells" from *Collected Poems* by Thomas Hardy, Copyright 1925 by The Macmillan Company, renewed 1953 by Lloyds Bank, Ltd.; for "What the Moon Saw" from *Collected Poems* by Vachel Lindsay, Copyright 1914 by The Macmillan Company, renewed 1942 by Elizabeth C. Lindsay; and for "For Anne Gregory" from *Collected Poems* by William Butler Yeats, Copyright 1933 by The Macmillan Company, renewed 1961 by Bertha Georgie Yeats.

THE MACMILLAN COMPANY OF CANADA LIMITED, MACMILLAN LONDON AND BASINGSTOKE, and THE TRUSTEES OF THE HARDY ESTATE for "Inscription for a Peal of Eight Bells" and "Cynic's Epitaph" from the *Collected Poems of Thomas Hardy*.

WILLIAM MORROW AND COMPANY, INC., for "The Prayer of Cyrus Brown" from *Dreams in Homespun* by Sam Walter Foss, reprinted by permission of Lothrop, Lee & Shepard Co.

NEW DIRECTIONS PUBLISHING CORPORATION for "Nature's Gentleman" from *Long Live Man* by Gregory Corso, Copyright © 1962 by New Directions Publishing Corporation; for "Fortunatus the R.A." by Nikarchos, "The Frugal Host" by Automedon, "Meditation on Beavers" by Lucian of Samosata, "On Apis the Prizefighter" by Lucilius, "On a School-Teacher," "On Mauros the Rhetor" by Palladas, "On Torpid Marcus" by Lucilius, "To a Friend: Constructive Criticism"

To Irene and Leon Livingston

CONTENTS

WHAT A WONDERFUL BIRD
THE FROG ARE

THE FROG

What a wonderful bird the frog are—
When he stand he sit almost;
When he hop, he fly almost.
He ain't got no sense hardly;
He ain't got no tail hardly either.
When he sit, he sit on what he ain't got almost.

Anonymous

A beautiful lady named Psyche
Is loved by a fellow named Yche.
  One thing about Ych
  The lady can't lych
Is his beard, which is dreadfully spyche.

Anonymous

A decrepit old gasman, named Peter,
While hunting around for the meter,
  Touched a leak with his light;
  He rose out of sight—
And, as anyone who knows anything
  about poetry can tell you,
  he also ruined the meter.

Anonymous

Amelia mixed the mustard,
    She mixed it good and thick;
She put it in the custard
    And made her Mother sick,
And showing satisfaction
    By many a loud huzza
"Observe" said she "the action
    Of mustard on Mamma."

A. E. Housman

THE ARTIST

The Artist and his Luckless Wife
They lead a horrid haunted life,
Surrounded by the things he's made
That are not wanted by the trade.

The world is very fair to see;
The Artist will not let it be;
He fiddles with the works of God,
And makes them look uncommon odd.

The Artist is an awful man,
He does not do the things he can;
He does the things he cannot do,
And we attend the private view.

The Artist uses honest paint
To represent things as they ain't,
He then asks money for the time
It took to perpetrate the crime.

Sir Walter Raleigh

AUNT ELIZA

In the drinking-well
    Which the plumber built her,
Aunt Eliza fell . . .
    . . . We must buy a filter.

Harry Graham

BETTER COME QUIETLY

From *Six Theological Cradle Songs**

Baby John: O kinsfolk and gentlefolk, PLEASE be forgiving,
But nothing can lure me to living, to living.
I'm snug where I am; I don't WISH to burst
through.
Chorus of Nurses, Furies, & Muses:
That's what YOU think. If only you KNEW.

Baby John: Well then YES, I'll be BORN, but my EARTH
will be heaven;
My dice will throw nothing but seven-eleven;
Life is tall lilacs, all giddy with dew.
Chorus of Nurses, Furies, & Muses:
That's what YOU think. If only you KNEW.

Baby John: Well then YES, there'll be sorrows, be sorrows
that best me;
But these are mere teasings to test me, to test me.
We'll ZOOM from our graves when God orders
us to.
Chorus of Nurses, Furies, & Muses:
That's what YOU think. If only you KNEW.

Baby John: Well then YES, I'll belie my belief in survival.
But IF there's no God, then at least there's no
devil:

If at LAST I must die—well, at LEAST when
    I do,
It's clear I won't sizzle.
Chorus of Nurses, Furies, & Muses:
                    If only you KNEW.

* Composed for my son's christening, 1946. The capitalizations
. . . imitate the bounce and emphasis of a child chanting while
stamping on the springs of his crib.

Peter Viereck

BRINGING HIM UP

(to be read solemnly)

Mister Thomas Jones
Said to James, his son:
"Never swallow bones,
Never point a gun.

Never slam a door,
Never play with flames,
Never shun the poor."
"Dull old fool!" said James.

Lord Dunsany

THE BUILDERS

I told them a thousand times if I told them once:
Stop fooling around, I said, with straw and sticks;
They won't hold up. You're taking an awful chance.
Brick is the stuff to build with, solid bricks.
You want to be impractical, go ahead.
But just remember, I told them; wait and see,
You're making a big mistake. Awright, I said,
But when the wolf comes, don't come running to me.

The funny thing is, they didn't. There they sat,
One in his crummy yellow shack, and one
Under his roof of twigs, and the wolf ate
Them, hair and hide. Well, what is done is done.
But I'd been willing to help them, all along,
If only they'd once admitted they were wrong.

Sara Henderson Hay

BUNTHORNE'S SONG

Sung by Reginald Bunthorne (A Fleshly Poet) in *Patience*

If you're anxious for to shine in the high aesthetic line as a
    man of culture rare,
You must get up all the germs of the transcendental terms, and
    plant them everywhere.
You must lie upon the daisies, and discourse in novel phrases
    of your complicated state of mind,
The meaning doesn't matter if it's only idle chatter of a
    transcendental kind.
                And every one will say,
                As you walk your mystic way,
"If this young man expresses himself in terms too deep for *me,*
Why, what a very singularly deep young man this deep young
    man must be!"

Be eloquent in praise of the very dull old days which have long
    since passed away,
And convince 'em, if you can, that the reign of good Queen
    Anne was Culture's palmiest day.
Of course you will pooh-pooh whatever's fresh and new, and
    declare it's crude and mean,
For Art stopped short in the cultivated court of the Empress
    Josephine.
                And every one will say,
                As you walk your mystic way,
"If that's not good enough for him which is good enough for
    me,
Why, what a very cultivated kind of youth this kind of youth
    must be!"

30

Then a sentimental passion of a vegetable fashion must excite
your languid spleen,
An attachment *à la* Plato for a bashful young potato, or a not-
too-French French bean!
Though the Philistines may jostle, you will rank as an apostle
in the high aesthetic band,
If you walk down Piccadilly with a poppy or a lily in your
mediaeval hand.
       And every one will say,
       As you walk your flowery way,
"If he's content with a vegetable love which would certainly
not suit *me,*
Why, what a most particularly pure young man this pure
young man must be!"

W. S. Gilbert

THE CHEMIST TO HIS LOVE

I love thee, Mary, and thou lovest me—
Our mutual flame is like th' affinity
That doth exist between two simple bodies:
I am Potassium to thine Oxygen.
'Tis little that the holy marriage vow
Shall shortly make us one. That unity
Is, after all, but metaphysical.
Oh, would that I, my Mary, were an acid,
A living acid; thou an alkali
Endow'd with human sense, that, brought together,
We both might coalesce into one salt,
One homogeneous crystal. Oh, that thou
Wert Carbon, and myself were Hydrogen;
We would unite to form olefiant gas,
Or common coal, or naphtha—would to heaven
That I were Phosphorous, and thou wert Lime!
And we of Lime composed a Phosphuret.
I'd be content to be Sulphuric Acid,
So that thou might be Soda. In that case
We should be Glauber's Salt. Wert thou Magnesia
Instead we'd form the salt that's named from Epsom.
Our happy union should that compound form,
Nitrate of Potash—otherwise Salpetre.
And thus our several natures sweetly blent,
We'd live and love together, until death
Should decompose the fleshly tertium quid,

Leaving our souls to all eternity
Amalgamated. Sweet, thy name is Briggs
And mine is Johnson. Wherefore should not we
Agree to form a Johnsonate of Briggs?

Anonymous

COSSIMBAZAR

Come fleetly, come fleetly, my hookabadar,
For the sound of the tam-tam is heard from afar.
"Banoolah! Banoolah!" The Brahmins are nigh,
And the depths of the jungle re-echo their cry.
                Pestonjee Bomanjee!
                Smite the guitar;
Join in the chorus, my hookabadar.

Heed not the blast of the deadly monsoon,
Nor the blue Brahmaputra that gleams in the moon.
Stick to thy music, or oh, let the sound
Be heard with distinctness a mile or two round.
                Jamsetjee, Jeejeebhoy!
                Sweep the guitar.
Join in the chorus, my hookabadar.

Art thou a Buddhist, or dost thou indeed
Put faith in the monstrous Mohammedan creed?
Art thou a Ghebir—a blinded Parsee?
Not that it matters an atom to me.
                Cursetjee Bomanjee!
                Twang the guitar
Join in the chorus, my hookabadar.

                                Henry S. Leigh

THE CUMMERBUND

An Indian Poem

I

She sate upon her Dobie,
    To watch the Evening Star,
And all the Punkahs, as they passed,
    Cried, "My! how fair you are!"
Around her bower, with quivering leaves,
    The tall Kamsamahs grew,
And Kitmutgars in wild festoons
    Hung down from Tchokis blue.

II

Below her home the river rolled
    With soft meloobious sound,
Where golden-finned Chuprassies swam,
    In myriads circling round.
Above, on tallest trees remote,
    Green Ayahs perched alone,
And all night long the Mussak moan'd
    Its melancholy tone.

III

And where the purple Nullahs threw
    Their branches far and wide,
And silvery Goreewallahs flew
    In silence, side by side,
The little Bheesties' twittering cry

Rose on the fragrant air,
And oft the angry Jampan howled
    Deep in his hateful lair.

IV

She sate upon her Dobie,
    She heard the Nimmak hum,
When all at once a cry arose,
    "The Cummerbund is come!"
In vain she fled: with open jaws
    The angry monster followed,
And so (before assistance came)
    That Lady Fair was swollowed.

V

They sought in vain for even a bone
    Respectfully to bury;
They said, "Hers was a dreadful fate!"
    (And Echo answered, "Very.")
They nailed her Dobie to the wall,
    Where last her form was seen,
And underneath they wrote these words,
    In yellow, blue, and green:

"Beware, ye Fair! Ye Fair, beware!
    Nor sit out late at night,
Lest horrid Cummerbunds should come,
    And swollow you outright."

                    Edward Lear

CYNIC'S EPITAPH

A race with the sun as he downed
    I ran at evetide,
Intent who should first gain the ground
    And there hide.

He beat me by some minutes then,
    But I triumphed anon,
For when he'd to rise again
    I stayed on.

Thomas Hardy

DINKY

O what's the weather in a Beard?
It's windy there, and rather weird,
And when you think the sky has cleared
   —Why, there is Dirty Dinky.

Suppose you walk out in a Storm,
With nothing on to keep you warm,
And then step barefoot on a Worm
   —Of course, it's Dirty Dinky.

As I was crossing a hot hot Plain,
I saw a sight that caused me pain,
You asked me before, I'll tell you again:
   —It *looked* like Dirty Dinky.

Last night you lay a-sleeping? No!
The room was thirty-five below;
The sheets and blankets turned to snow.
   —He'd got in: Dirty Dinky.

You'd better watch the things you do.
You'd better watch the things you do.
You're part of him; he's part of you
   —*You* may be Dirty Dinky.

Theodore Roethke

THE DINOSAUR

Behold the mighty Dinosaur,
Famous in prehistoric lore,
Not only for his weight and strength
But for his intellectual length.
You will observe by these remains
The creature had two sets of brains—
One in his head (the usual place),
The other at his spinal base.
Thus he could reason *a priori*
As well as *a posteriori*.
No problem bothered him a bit:
He made both head and tail of it.
So wise was he, so wise and solemn,
Each thought filled just a spinal column.
If one brain found the pressure strong
It passed a few ideas along;
If something slipped his forward mind
'Twas rescued by the one behind;
And if in error he was caught
He had a saving afterthought.
As he thought twice before he spoke
He had no judgments to revoke;
For he could think, without congestion,
Upon both sides of every question.

Oh, gaze upon this model beast,
Defunct, ten million years at least.

Bert Leston Taylor

ELEGY

The jackals prowl, the serpents hiss
In what was once Persepolis.
Proud Babylon is but a trace
Upon the desert's dusty face.
The topless towers of Ilium
Are ashes. Judah's harp is dumb.
The fleets of Nineveh and Tyre
Are down with Davy Jones, Esquire
And all the oligarchies, kings,
And potentates that ruled these things
Are gone! But cheer up! don't be sad;
Think what a lovely time they had!

Arthur Guiterman

AN ELEGY ON THE DEATH OF
A MAD DOG

Good people all, of every sort,
    Give ear unto my song;
And if you find it wondrous short,—
    It cannot hold you long.

In Islington there was a man
    Of whom the world might say
That still a godly race he ran,—
    Whene'er he went to pray.

A kind and gentle heart he had,
    To comfort friends and foes;
The naked every day he clad,—
    When he put on his clothes.

And in that town a dog was found,
    As many dogs there be,
Both mongrel, puppy, whelp, and hound,
    And curs of low degree.

The dog and man at first were friends;
    But when a pique began,
The dog, to gain some private ends,
    Went mad, and bit the man.

Around from all the neighboring streets,
    The wondering neighbors ran,
And swore the dog had lost his wits
    To bite so good a man.

The wound it seemed both sore and sad
    To every Christian eye;
And while they swore the dog was mad
    They swore the man would die.

But soon a wonder came to light,
    That showed the rogues they lied;
The man recovered of the bite,
    The dog it was that died.

Oliver Goldsmith

THE ELEPHANT, OR
THE FORCE OF HABIT

A tail behind, a trunk in front
Complete the usual elephant.
The tail in front, the trunk behind
Is what you very seldom find.

If you for specimens should hunt
With trunks behind and tails in front,
That hunt would occupy you long;
The force of habit is so strong.

A. E. Housman

AN EMPTY HOUSE

You beat your Pate, and fancy Wit will come:
Knock as you please, there's nobody at home.

Alexander Pope

EPITAPH FOR A POSTAL CLERK

Here lies wrapped up tight in sod,
Henry Harkins c/o God.
On the day of Resurrection,
May be opened for inspection.

X. J. Kennedy

EPITAPH IN ELGIN CATHEDRAL

Here lie I, Martin Elginbrodde:
Ha'e mercy o' my soul, Lord God,
As I wad do, were I Lord God
And ye were Martin Elginbrodde.

Unknown

EPITAPH ON CHARLES II

Here lies our Sovereign Lord the King,
 Whose word no man relies on,
Who never said a foolish thing,
 Nor ever did a wise one.

John Wilmot, Earl of Rochester

AN EXPOSTULATION

When late I attempted your pity to move,
    What made you so deaf to my prayers?
Perhaps it was right to dissemble your love,
    But—why did you kick me downstairs?

Isaac Bickerstaff
(Pseudonymn of Jonathan Swift)

THE FIREFLY

The firefly's flame
Is something for which science has no name.
I can think of nothing eerier
Than flying around with an unidentified glow on a person's
    posteerier.

Ogden Nash

FOR A LADY I KNOW

She even thinks that up in heaven
    Her class lies late and snores,
While poor black cherubs rise at seven
    To do celestial chores.

Countee Cullen

FOR ANNE GREGORY

'Never shall a young man,
Thrown into despair
By those great honey-coloured
Ramparts at your ear,
Love you for yourself alone
And not your yellow hair.'

'But I can get a hair-dye
And set such colour there,
Brown, or black, or carrot,
That young men in despair
May love me for myself alone
And not my yellow hair.'

'I heard an old religious man
But yesternight declare
That he had found a text to prove
That only God, my dear,
Could love you for yourself alone
And not your yellow hair.'

W. B. Yeats

FORTUNATUS THE R.A.

Fortunatus the portrait-painter got twenty sons
But never one likeness.

> *Nikarchos*
> Translated by Dudley Fitts

THE FRUGAL HOST

My dinner yesterday was the shin of an elderly goat
And a serving of hempen cabbage ten days cut.
My host's name? I'll not tell you:
He's an irritable chap, and might invite me again!

> *Automedon*
> Translated by Dudley Fitts

GLOSS

I know a little man both ept and ert.
An intro-? extro-? No, he's just a vert.
Sheveled and couth and kempt, pecunious, ane,
His image trudes upon the ceptive brain.

When life turns sipid and the mind is traught,
The spirit soars as I would sist it ought.
Chalantly then, like any gainly goof,
My digent self is sertive, choate, loof.

David McCord

THE GNU

There's *this* to Remember about the Gnu:
He *closely* Resembles—but I *can't* tell *you!*

Theodore Roethke

GOO-GIRL

Poor Myrtle would sigh, "Sweet my Coz,
The *Things* you do, Nobody does:
Putting Egg in your Shoe
And then making Goo,
Which, with Slobbers and Snorts,
You drink up in Quarts;
And that Gravy and Fat
All over your Hat,—
How *Did* you do *That?*
When you Slurp, and go, Poof!
The Cat runs for a Roof
Clear under the Chair;
And your Friends,—how they Stare!
The Mere Mention of Soups
Makes them Huddle in Groups,—
And they'll soon stay away in Great Bunches!"

Theodore Roethke

THE GREAT AUK'S GHOST

The Greak Auk's ghost rose on one leg,
  Sighed thrice and three times winkt,
And turned and poached a phantom egg,
  And muttered, 'I'm extinct.'

Ralph Hodgson

HAEC FABULA DOCET

A Blindman by the name of La Fontaine,
Relying on himself and on his cane,
Came tap-tap-tapping down the village street,
The apogee of human blind conceit.
Now just ahead of him was seen to yawn
A trench where water pipes were laying on.
The Blindman might have found it with his ferrule,
But someone overanxious at his peril
Not only warned him with a loud command
But ran against him with a staying hand.
Enraged at what he could but think officious,
The Blindman missed him with a blow so vicious
He gave his own poor iliac a wrench
And plunged himself head foremost in the trench:
Where with a glee no less for being grim
The workmen all turned to and buried him.

Moral

The moral is, it hardly need be shown,
All those who try to go it sole alone,
Too proud to be beholden for relief,
Are absolutely sure to come to grief.

Robert Frost

'Hallelujah!' was the only observation
That escaped Lieutenant-Colonel Mary Jane,
When she tumbled off the platform in the station,
And was cut in little pieces by the train.
      Mary Jane, the train is through yer:
      Hallelujah! Hallelujah!
We will gather up the fragments that remain.

A. E. Housman

Note: When the Salvation Army was becoming a prominent movement in England, A. E. Housman wrote this. See also "There is Hallelujah Hannah."

THE HEADLESS GARDENER

A gardener, Tobias Baird,
sent his head to be repaired;
he thought, as nothing much was wrong,
he wouldn't be without it long.

Ten years he's weeded path and plot,
a headless gardener, God wot,
always hoping (hope is vain)
to see his noddle back again.

Don't pity him for his distress—
he never sent up his address.

Ian Serraillier

THE HEN AND THE CARP

Once, in a roostery
there lived a speckled hen, and when-
ever she laid an egg this hen
ecstatically cried:
'O progeny miraculous, particular spectaculous,
what a wonderful hen am I!'

Down in a pond nearby
perchance a fat and broody carp
was basking, but her ears were sharp—
she heard Dame Cackle cry:
'O progeny miraculous, particular spectaculous,
what a wonderful hen am I!'

'Ah, Cackle,' bubbled she,
'for your single egg, O silly one,
I lay at least a million;
suppose for each I cried:
"O progeny miraculous, particular spectaculous!"
what a hullaballoo there'd be!'

Ian Serraillier

Here lies old Jones,
Who all his life collected bones,
Till death, that grim and bony spectre,
That all-amassing bone collector,
Boned old Jones, so neat and tidy,
That here he lies all bona fide.

Anonymous

Higgledy-piggledy
Ludwig van Beethoven
Bored by request for some
Music to hum,

Finally answered with
Oversimplicity,
"Here's my fifth symphony:
Duh, duh, duh, DUM!"

E. William Seaman

HISTORICAL REFLECTIONS

Higgledy-piggledy,
Benjamin Harrison
Twenty-third President
Was, and, as such,

Served between Clevelands, and
Save for this trivial
Idiosyncracy,
Didn't do much.

John Hollander

I knew a Cappadocian
Who fell into the Ocean:
His mother came and took him out
With tokens of emotion!

She also had a daughter
Who fell into the Water:
At any rate she would have fallen
If someone hadn't caught her.

The second son went frantic
And fell in the Atlantic:
His parent reached the spot too late
To check her offspring's antic.

Her grief was then terrific:
She fell in the Pacific,
Exclaiming with her latest breath
"I have been too prolific."

A. E. Housman

I MARVEL AT THE WAYS OF GOD

I marvel at the ways of God,
    For time and time again
I see Him paint such lovely clouds
    Above such awkward men.

E. B. White

If things were better
for me, flies, I'd invite you
    to share my supper.

Issa
Translated by Harry Behn

IF YOU HAVE SEEN

Good reader! if you e'er have seen,
  When Phoebus hastens to his pillow,
The mermaids, with their tresses green,
  Dancing upon the western billow:
If you have seen, at twilight dim,
When the lone spirit's vesper hymn
  Floats wild along the winding shore:
If you have seen, through mist of eve,
The fairy train their ringlets weave,
Glancing along the spangled green;—
  If you have seen all this and more,
God bless me! What a deal you've seen!

Thomas Moore

AN IMPORTER

Mrs. Someone's been to Asia.
What she brought back would amaze ye.
Bamboos, ivories, jades, and lacquers,
Devil-scaring firecrackers,
Recipes for tea with butter,
Sacred rigmaroles to mutter,
Subterfuge for saving faces,
A developed taste in vases,
Arguments too stale to mention
'Gainst American invention—
Most of all the mass production
Destined to prove our destruction.
What are telephones, skyscrapers,
Safety razors, Sunday papers
But the silliest evasion
Of the truths we owe an Asian?
But the best of her exhibit
Was a prayer machine from Tibet
That by brook power in the garden
Kept repeating Pardon, pardon;
And as picturesque machinery
Beat a sundial in the scenery—
The most primitive of engines
Mass-producing with a vengeance.
Teach those Asians mass production?
Teach your grandmother egg suction.

Robert Frost

'In the back back garden, Thomasina
  Did you recently vociferate a squeal?'
'Oh, I trod upon an amphisbaena,
  And it bit me on the toe and on the heel.
    Yes, it bit me (do you know)
    With its tail upon the toe,
  While it bit me with its head upon the heel!'

'How excessively distracting and confusing.
  Pray what, Thomasina, did you do?'
'Oh, I took the garden scissors I was using
  And I snipped it irretrievably in two.
    And it split with such a scrunch
    That I shall not want my lunch,
  And if you had heard the noise no more would you.'

'And where, Thomasina, are the sections
  Of the foe that you courageously repressed?'
'Oh, they ran away in opposite directions,
  And they vanished in the east and in the west.
    And the way they made me squint,
    It would melt a heart of flint,
  And I think that I will go upstairs and rest.'

                                        A. E. Housman

INCIDENTS IN THE LIFE OF
MY UNCLE ARLY

I

O my agèd Uncle Arly!
Sitting on a heap of Barley
     Thro' the silent hours of night,—
Close beside a leafy thicket:—
On his nose there was a Cricket,—
In his hat a Railway-Ticket;—
     (But his shoes were far too tight.)

II

Long ago, in youth, he squander'd
All his goods away, and wander'd
     To the Tiniskoop-hills afar.
There on golden sunsets blazing,
Every evening found him gazing,—
Singing,—"Orb! you're quite amazing!
     How I wonder what you are!"

III

Like the ancient Medes and Persians,
Always by his own exertions
     He subsisted on those hills;—
Whiles,—by teaching children spelling,—
Or at times by merely yelling,—
Or at intervals by selling
     "Propter's Nicodemus Pills."

IV

Later, in his morning rambles
He perceived the moving brambles—
    Something square and white disclose;—
'Twas a First-class Railway Ticket;
But, on stooping down to pick it
Off the ground,—a pea-green Cricket
    Settled on my uncle's Nose.

V

Never—never more,—oh! never,
Did that Cricket leave him ever,—
    Dawn or evening, day or night;—
Clinging as a constant treasure,—
Chirping with a cheerious measure,—
Wholly to my uncle's pleasure,—
    (Though his shoes were far too tight.)

VI

So for three-and-forty winters,
Till his shoes were worn to splinters,
    All those hills he wander'd o'er,—
Sometimes silent;—sometimes yelling;—
Till he came to Borley-Melling,
Near his old ancestral dwelling;—
    (But his shoes were far too tight.)

On a little heap of Barley
Died my agèd uncle Arly,
    And they buried him one night;—
Close beside the leafy thicket;—
There,—his hat and Railway-Ticket;—
There,—his ever-faithful Cricket;—
    (But his shoes were far too tight.)

Edward Lear

INSCRIPTION FOR A PEAL OF EIGHT BELLS

After a Restoration

I.   Thomas Tremble new-made me
        Eighteen hundred and fifty-three;
        Why he did I fail to see.

II.   I was well-toned by William Brine,
        Seventeen hundred and twenty-nine;
        Now, recast, I weakly whine!

III.   Fifteen hundred used to be
        My date, but since they melted me
        'Tis only eighteen fifty-three.

IV.   Henry Hopkins got me made,
        And I summon folk as bade;
        Not to much purpose, I'm afraid.

V.   Likewise; for I bang and bid
        In commoner metal than I did,
        Some of me being stolen and hid.

VI.   I, too, since in a mould they flung me,
        Drained my silver, and rehung me,
        So that in tin-like tones I tongue me.

VII. In nineteen hundred, so 'tis said,
        They cut my canon off my head,
        And made me look scalped, scraped and dead.

VIII. I'm the peal's tenor still, but rue it!
Once it took two to swing me through it;
Now I'm rehung, one dolt can do it.

Thomas Hardy

I

INTENDED FOR SIR ISAAC NEWTON

In Westminster Abbey

ISAACUS NEWTONUS

QUEM IMMORTALEM TESTANTUR TEMPUS,
NATURA, COELUM: MORTALEM HOC
MARMOR FATETUR

Nature and Nature's laws lay hid in Night:
God said, *Let* NEWTON *be!* and all was Light.

Alexander Pope

II

It did not last: the Devil, howling *Ho!*
Let Einstein be! restored the status quo.

J. C. Squire

INTERVIEW

Yes, this is where she lived before she won
The title Miss Glass Slipper of the Year,
And went to the ball and married the king's son.
You're from the local press, and want to hear
About her early life? Young man, sit down.
These are my *own* two daughters; you'll not find
Nicer, more biddable girls in all the town,
And lucky, I tell them, not to be the kind

That Cinderella was, spreading those lies,
Telling those shameless tales about the way
We treated her. Oh, nobody denies
That she was pretty, if you like those curls.
But looks aren't everything, I always say.
Be sweet and natural, I tell my girls,
And Mr. Right will come along, some day.

Sara Henderson Hay

JABBERWOCKY

'Twas brillig, and the slithy toves
　　Did gyre and gimble in the wabe:
All mimsy were the borogoves,
　　And the mome raths outgrabe.

"Beware the Jabberwock, my son!
　　The jaws that bite, the claws that catch!
Beware the Jubjub bird, and shun
　　The frumious Bandersnatch!"

He took his vorpal sword in hand:
　　Long time the manxome foe he sought—
So rested he by the Tumtum tree,
　　And stood awhile in thought.

And as in uffish thought he stood,
　　The Jabberwock, with eyes of flame,
Came whiffling through the tulgey wood,
　　And burbled as it came!

One, two! One, two! And through and through
　　The vorpal blade went snicker-snack!
He left it dead, and with its head
　　He went galumphing back.

"And, hast thou slain the Jabberwock?
　　Come to my arms, my beamish boy!
O frabjous day! Callooh! Callay!"
　　He chortled in his joy.

'Twas brillig, and the slithy toves
  Did gyre and gimble in the wabe:
All mimsy were the borogoves,
  And the mome raths outgrabe.

Lewis Carroll

Note: Lewis Carroll, in 1855, wrote the following explanation of
"Stanza of Anglo-Saxon Poetry":

> *Twas bryllyg, and the slythy toves*
> *Did gyre and gymble in ye wabe:*
> *All mimsy were ye borogoves;*
> *And ye mome raths outgrabe.*

This curious fragment reads thus in modern characters:

> *'Twas bryllyg, and the slythy toves*
> *Did gyre and gymble in the wabe:*
> *All mimsy were the borogoves;*
> *And the mome raths outgrabe.*

The meanings of the words are as follows:

Bryllyg (derived from the verb to *bryl* or *broil*). 'The time of
broiling dinner, i.e. the close of the afternoon!'

Slythy (compounded of *slimy* and *lithe*). 'Smooth and active.'

Tove. A species of Badger. They had smooth white hair, long
hind legs, and short horns like a stag; lived chiefly on cheese.

Gyre. Verb (derived from *gyaour* or *giaour,* 'a dog'). 'To scratch
like a dog.'

Gymble (whence *gimblet*). 'To screw out holes in anything.'

Wabe (derived from the verb to *swab* or *soak*). 'The side of hill' (from its being soaked by the rain).

Mimsy (whence *mimserable* and *miserable*). 'Unhappy.'

Borogove. An extinct kind of Parrot. They had no wings, beaks turned up, and made their nests under sun-dials; lived on veal.

Mome (hence *solemome, solemone,* and *solemn*). 'Grave.'

Rath. A species of land turtle. Head erect; mouth like a shark; forelegs curved out so that the animal walked on its knees; smooth green body; lived on swallows and oysters.

Outgrabe, past tense of the verb to *outgribe.* (It is connected with old verb to *grike* or *shrike,* from which are derived 'shriek' and 'creak.') 'Squeaked.'

Hence the literal English of the passage is:
'It was evening, and the smooth active badgers were scratching and boring holes in the hill-side; all unhappy were the parrots; and the grave turtles squeaked out.'

There were probably sundials on the top of the hill, and the 'borogoves' were afraid that their nests would be undermined. The hill was probably full of the nests of 'raths,' which ran out, squeaking with fear, on hearing the 'toves' scratching outside. This is an obscure, but yet deeply-affecting, relic of ancient Poetry.

CROFT 1855

JOHN BUN

Here lies John Bun.
He was killed by a gun.
His name was not Bun, but Wood,
But Wood would not rhyme with gun, but Bun would.

Anonymous

JOHNNY DOW

     Wha lies here?
I, Johnny Dow.
Hoo! Johnny is that you?
Ay, man, but a'm dead now.

Anonymous

KIND OF AN ODE TO DUTY

O Duty,
Why hast thou not the visage of a sweetie or a cutie?
Why displayest thou the countenance of the kind of
    conscientious organizing spinster
That the minute you see her you are aginster?
Why glitter thy spectacles so ominously?
Why art thou clad so abominously?
Why art thou so different from Venus
And why do thou and I have so few interests mutually in
    common between us?
Why art thou fifty per cent martyr
And fifty-one per cent Tartar?
Why is it thy unfortunate wont
To try to attract people by calling on them either to leave
    undone the deeds they like, or to do the deeds they don't?
Why art thou so like an April post mortem
On something that died in autumn?
Above all, why dost thou continue to hound me?
Why art thou always albatrossly hanging around me?
Thou so ubiquitous,
And I so iniquitous.
I seem to be the one person in the world thou art perpetually
    preaching at who or to who;
Whatever looks like fun, there art thou standing between me
    and it, calling yoo-hoo.
O Duty, Duty!
How noble a man should I be hadst thou the visage of a
    sweetie or a cutie!
Wert thou but houri instead of hag
Then would my halo indeed be in the bag!

But as it is thou art so much forbiddinger than a Wodehouse
　　hero's forbiddingest aunt
That in the words of the poet, When Duty whispers low, Thou
　　must, this erstwhile youth replies, I just can't.

Ogden Nash

KING TUT

King Tut
Crossed over the Nile
On steppingstones of crocodile.

King Tut!
His mother said,
Come here this minute!
You'll get wet feet.
King Tut is dead

And now King Tut
Tight as a nut
Keeps his big fat Mummy shut.

King Tut,
       tut, tut.

X. J. Kennedy

LAO-TZŬ

From *The Philosophers*

"Those who speak know nothing;
  Those who know are silent."
These words, as I am told,
Were spoken by Lao-tzŭ.
If we are to believe that Lao-tzŭ
    Was himself *one who knew,*
How comes it that he wrote a book
    Of five thousand words?

> *Po Chü-i*
> Translated by Arthur Waley

THE LESSER LYNX

The laughter of the lesser Lynx
　　Is often insincere:
It pays to be polite, he thinks,
　　If Royalty is near.

So when the Lion steals his food
　　Or kicks him from behind,
He smiles, of course—but oh, the rude
　　Remarks that cross his mind!

　　　　　　　　E. V. Rieu

LINES BY AN OLD FOGY

I'm thankful that the sun and moon
    Are both hung up so high,
That no presumptuous hand can stretch
    And pull them from the sky.
If they were not, I have no doubt
    But some reforming ass
Would recommend to take them down
    And light the world with gas.

Anonymous

MARY'S GHOST

A Pathetic Ballad

'Twas in the middle of the night,
   To sleep young William tried;
When Mary's Ghost came stealing in,
   And stood at his bed-side.

O William dear! O William dear!
   My rest eternal ceases;
Alas! my everlasting peace
   Is broken into pieces.

I thought the last of all my cares
   Would end with my last minute;
But though I went to my long home,
   I didn't stay long in it.

The body-snatchers they have come,
   And made a snatch at me;
It's very hard them kind of men
   Won't let a body be!

You thought that I was buried deep,
   Quite decent like and chary,
But from her grave in Mary-bone,
   They've come and boned your Mary.

The arm that used to take your arm
    Is took to Dr. Vyse;
And both my legs are gone to walk
    The hospital at Guy's.

I vowed that you should have my hand,
    But fate gives us denial;
You'll find it there, at Dr. Bell's,
    In spirits and a phial.

As for my feet, the little feet
    You used to call so pretty,
There's one, I know, in Bedford Row,
    The t'other's in the City.

I can't tell where my head is gone,
    But Dr. Carpue can;
As for my trunk, it's all packed up
    To go by Pickford's van.

I wish you'd go to Mr. P.
    And save me such a ride;
I don't half like the outside place,
    They've took for my inside.

The cock it crows—I must be gone!
    My William, we must part!
But I'll be yours in death, although
    Sir Astley has my heart.

Don't go to weep upon my grave,
    And think that there I be;
They haven't left an atom there
    Of my anatomie.

Thomas Hood

MEDITATIO

When I carefully consider the curious habits of dogs
I am compelled to conclude
That man is the superior animal.

When I consider the curious habits of man
I confess, my friend, I am puzzled.

Ezra Pound

MEDITATION ON BEAVERS

O lovely Whiskers, O inspirational Mop!
But if growing a beard, my friend, means acquiring wisdom,
Any old goat can be Plato.

Lucian of Samosata
Translated by Dudley Fitts

THE MICROBE

The Microbe is so very small
You cannot make him out at all,
But many sanguine people hope
To see him through a microscope.
His jointed tongue that lies beneath
A hundred curious rows of teeth;
His seven tufted tails with lots
Of lovely pink and purple spots,
On each of which a pattern stands,
Composed of forty separate bands;
His eyebrows of a tender green;
All these have never yet been seen—
But Scientists, who ought to know,
Assure us that they must be so . . .
Oh! let us never, never doubt
What nobody is sure about!

Hilaire Belloc

THE MICROSCOPE

Anton Leeuwenhoek was Dutch.
He sold pincushions, cloth, and such.
The waiting townsfolk fumed and fussed
As Anton's dry goods gathered dust.

He worked instead of tending store,
At grinding special lenses for
A microscope. Some of the things
He looked at were:
                              mosquitoes' wings,
the hairs of sheep, the legs of lice,
the skin of people, dogs, and mice;
ox eyes, spiders' spinning gear,
fishes' scales, a little smear
of his own blood,
                              and best of all
the unknown, busy, very small
bugs that swim and bump and hop
inside a simple water drop.

Impossible! Most Dutchmen said.
This Anton's crazy in the head.
We ought to ship him off to Spain.
He says he's seen a housefly's brain.
He says the water that we drink
Is full of bugs. He's mad, we think!

They called him dumkopf which means dope.
That's how we got the microscope.

Maxine Kumin

86

MIDSUMMER MELANCHOLY

Oh, somewhere there are people who
Have nothing in the world to do
But sit upon the Pyrenees
And use the very special breeze
Provided for the people who
Have nothing in the world to do
But sit upon the Pyrenees
And use the . . .

Margaret Fishback

MOTHER GOOSE'S GARLAND

Around, around the sun we go:
The moon goes round the earth.
We do not die of death:
We die of vertigo.

Archibald MacLeish

MUSEUM PIECE

The good gray guardians of art
Patrol the halls on spongy shoes,
Impartially protective, though
Perhaps suspicious of Toulouse.

Here dozes one against the wall,
Disposed upon a funeral chair.
A Degas dancer pirouettes
Upon the parting of his hair.

See how she spins! The grace is there,
But strain as well is plain to see.
Degas loved the two together:
Beauty joined to energy.

Edgar Degas purchased once
A fine El Greco, which he kept
Against the wall beside his bed
To hang his pants on while he slept.

                    Richard Wilbur

My aunt kept turnips in a flock—
Did you ever hear of such strange stock?
They'd the funniest wool you ever did see;
It looked like turnip greens to me.

Turnip greens, oh turnip greens!
There's nothing I love like turnip greens!

Randall Jarrell

MY FACE

As a beauty I'm not a great star,
There are others more handsome by far,
But my face I don't mind it,
Because I'm behind it—
'Tis the folks in the front that I jar!

Anthony Euwer

THE NAMING OF CATS

The Naming of Cats is a difficult matter,
    It isn't just one of your holiday games;
You may think at first I'm as mad as a hatter
When I tell you, a cat must have THREE DIFFERENT NAMES.
First of all, there's the name that the family use daily,
    Such as Peter, Augustus, Alonzo or James,
Such as Victor or Jonathan, George or Bill Bailey—
    All of them sensible everyday names.
There are fancier names if you think they sound sweeter,
    Some for the gentlemen, some for the dames:
Such as Plato, Admetus, Electra, Demeter—
    But all of them sensible everyday names.
But I tell you, a cat needs a name that's particular,
    A name that's peculiar, and more dignified,
Else how can he keep up his tail perpendicular,
    Or spread out his whiskers, or cherish his pride?
Of names of this kind, I can give you a quorum,
    Such as Munkustrap, Quaxo, or Coricopat,
Such as Bombalurina, or else Jellylorum—
    Names that never belong to more than one cat.
But above and beyond there's still one name left over,
    And that is the name that you never will guess;
The name that no human research can discover—
    But THE CAT HIMSELF KNOWS, and will never confess.
When you notice a cat in profound meditation,
    The reason, I tell you, is always the same:

His mind is engaged in a rapt contemplation
    Of the thought, of the thought, of the thought of his name:
        His ineffable effable
        Effanineffable
Deep and inscrutable singular Name.

T. S. Eliot

NATURAL HISTORY

I wish I knew the reason for
The vegetarian dinosaur

That fed on ginkgo leaves and bran
Long before man-eating man;

That nibbled some narcotic tree
And nuzzled by an oozing sea;

Went unlamented to a grave
Below the Mesozoic wave

Long before ginkgo leaves and bran
Were eaten by man-eating man.

William Jay Smith

NATURE'S GENTLEMAN

My first English fog!
And come at the right time too!
Had a terrible night
      in which I cursed gentlemanliness

So out into it I go
      and ho the detective's hollow walk
Mary Dare? Art thou Mary Dare?
And banged straight into a tree
and said: Excuse me

              Gregory Corso

nobody loses all the time

i had an uncle named
Sol who was a born failure and
nearly everybody said he should have gone
into vaudeville perhaps because my Uncle Sol could
sing McCann He Was A Diver on Xmas Eve like Hell Itself
    which
may or may not account for the fact that my Uncle

Sol indulged in that possibly most inexcusable
of all to use a highfalootin phrase
luxuries that is or to
wit farming and be
it needlessly
added

my Uncle Sol's farm
failed because the chickens
ate the vegetables so
my Uncle Sol had a
chicken farm till the
skunks ate the chickens when

my Uncle Sol
had a skunk farm but
the skunks caught cold and
died and so
my Uncle Sol imitated the
skunks in a subtle manner

or by drowning himself in the watertank
but somebody who'd given my Uncle Sol a Victor
Victrola and records while he lived presented to
him upon the auspicious occasion of his decease a
scrumptious not to mention splendiferous funeral with
tall boys in black gloves and flowers and everything and

i remember we all cried like the Missouri
when my Uncle Sol's coffin lurched because
somebody pressed a button
(and down went
my Uncle
Sol

and started a worm farm)

e. e. cummings

NOTE TO MY NEIGHBOR

We might as well give up the fiction
    That we can argue any view.
For what in me is pure Conviction
    Is simple Prejudice in you.

Phyllis McGinley

"The sea is a subject by no means exhausted," A. E. Housman wrote in a letter. "I have somewhere a poem which directs attention to one of its most striking characteristics, which hardly any of the poets seem to have observed. They call it salt and blue and deep and dark and so on; but they never make such profoundly true reflexions as the following":

O billows bounding far,
How wet, how wet ye are!

When first my gaze ye met
I said 'Those waves are wet'.

I said it, and am quite
Convinced that I was right.

Who saith that ye are dry?
I give that man the lie.

Thy wetness, O thou sea,
Is wonderful to me.

It agitates my heart,
To think how wet thou art.

No object I have met
Is more profoundly wet.

Methinks 'twere vain to try,
O sea, to wipe thee dry.

I therefore will refrain.
Farwell, thou humid main.

A. E. Housman

O moon, why must you
inspire my neighbor to chirp
all night on a flute!

Koyo
Translated by Harry Behn

ODE TO THE AMOEBA

Recall from Time's abysmal chasm
That piece of primal protoplasm
The First Amoeba, strangely splendid,
From whom we're all of us descended.
That First Amoeba, weirdly clever,
Exists today and shall forever,
Because he reproduced by fission;
He split himself, and each division
And subdivision deemed it fitting
To keep on splitting, splitting, splitting;
So, whatsoe'er their billions be,
All, all amoebas still are he.
Zoologists discern his features
In every sort of breathing creatures,
Since all of every living species,
No matter how their breed increases
Or how their ranks have been recruited,
From him alone were evoluted.
King Solomon, the Queen of Sheba
And Hoover sprang from that amoeba;
Columbus, Shakespeare, Darwin, Shelley
Derived from that same bit of jelly.
So famed is he and well-connected,
His statue ought to be erected,
For you and I and William Beebe
Are undeniably amoebae!

Arthur Guiterman

ON A BAD SINGER

Swans sing before they die—'twere no bad thing
Should certain persons die before they sing.

Samuel Taylor Coleridge

ON A SCHOOL-TEACHER

Hail O ye seven pupils
Of Aristeidês the Rhetorician:

4 walls
& 3 settees.

Anonymous
Translated by Dudley Fitts

ON A SUNDIAL

I am a sundial, and I make a botch
Of what is done far better by a watch.

Hilaire Belloc

ON A WAITER

By and by
God caught his eye.

David McCord

ON *APIS THE PRIZEFIGHTER*

TO APIS THE BOXER
HIS GRATEFUL OPPONENTS HAVE ERECTED
THIS STATUE
HONORING HIM
WHO NEVER BY ANY CHANCE HURT ONE OF THEM

Lucilius
Translated by Dudley Fitts

ON MAUROS THE RHETOR

Lo, I beheld Mauros,
Professor of Public Speaking,
Raise high his elephant-snout
And from between his lips
(12 oz. apiece) give vent
To a voice whose very sound is accomplished murder.

I was impressed.

Palladas
Translated by Dudley Fitts

ON SIR JOHN VANBRUGH, ARCHITECT

Under this stone, reader, survey
Dead Sir John Vanbrugh's house of clay.
Lie heavy on him, earth! for he
Laid many heavy loads on thee.

Abel Evans

ON THE BIRTH OF HIS SON

Families, when a child is born
Want it to be intelligent.
I, through intelligence,
Having wrecked my whole life,
Only hope the baby will prove
Ignorant and stupid.
Then he will crown a tranquil life
By becoming a Cabinet Minister.

Su Tung-p'o
Translated by Arthur Waley

ON THE VANITY OF EARTHLY GREATNESS

The tusks that clashed in mighty brawls
Of mastodons, are billiard balls.

The sword of Charlemagne the Just
Is ferric oxide, known as rust.

The grizzly bear whose potent hug
Was feared by all, is now a rug.

Great Caesar's bust is on the shelf,
And I don't feel so well myself.

Arthur Guiterman

ON TORPID MARCUS

Lazy Marcus once dreamed he was running a race.
     (N.B.: He never went to bed again.)

Lucilius
Translated by Dudley Fitts

OPPORTUNITY

When Mrs. Gorm (Aunt Eloise)
Was stung to death by savage bees,
Her husband (Prebendary Gorm)
Put on his veil, and took the swarm.
He's publishing a book, next May,
On "How to Make Bee-keeping Pay."

Harry Graham

OVERHEARD IN THE LOUVRE

Said the Victory of Samothrace,
What winning's worth this loss of face?

X. J. Kennedy

PARSLEY FOR VICE-PRESIDENT

I'd like to be able to say a good word for parsley, but I can't,
And after all what can you find to say for something that even
    the dictionary dismisses as a biennial umbelliferous plant?
Speaking of which, I don't know how the dictionary figures it
    as biennial, it is biennial my eye, it is like the poor and the
    iniquitous,
Because it is always with us, because it is permanent and
    ubiquitous.
I will not venture to deny that it is umbelliferous,
I will only add that it is of a nasty green color, and faintly
    odoriferous,
And I hold by my complaint, though every cook and hostess
    in the land indict me for treason for it,
That parsley is something that as a rhymer I can find no
    rhyme for it and as an eater I can find no reason for it.
Well, there is one sin for which a lot of cooks and hostesses
    are some day going to have to atone,
Which is that they can't bear to cook anything and leave it
    alone.
No, they see food as something to base a lot of beautiful
    dreams and romance on,
Which explains lamb chops with pink and blue pants on.
Everything has to be all decorated and garnished
So the guests will be amazed and astarnished,
And whatever you get to eat, it's sprinkled with a lot of good
    old umbelliferous parsley looking as limp and as wistful as
    Lillian Gish,
And it is limpest, and wistfulest, and also thickest, on fish.
Indeed, I think maybe one reason for the disappearance of
    Enoch Arden

Was that his wife had an idea that mackerel tasted better if
    instead of looking like mackerel it looked like a garden.
Well, anyhow, there's the parsley cluttering up your food,
And the problem is to get it off without being rude,
And first of all you try to scrape it off with your fork,
And you might as well try to shave with a cork,
And then you surreptitiously try your fingers,
And you get covered with butter and gravy, but the parsley
    lingers,
And you turn red and smile at your hostess and compliment
    her on the recipe and ask her where she found it,
And then you return to the parsley and as a last resort you try
    to eat around it,
And the hostess says, Oh you are just picking at it, is there
    something wrong with it?
So all you can do is eat it all up, and the parsley along with it,
And now is the time for all good parsleyphobes to come to the
    aid of the menu and exhibit their gumption,
And proclaim that any dish that has either a taste or an
    appearance that can be improved by parsley is *ipso facto* a
    dish unfit for human consumption.

Ogden Nash

PASHA BAILEY BEN

A proud Pasha was BAILEY BEN,
His wives were three, his tails were ten;
His form was dignified, but stout,
Men called him "Little Roundabout."

His Importance

Pale pilgrims came from o'er the sea
To wait on PASHA BAILEY B.,
All bearing presents in a crowd,
For B. was poor as well as proud.

His Presents

They brought him onions strung on ropes,
And cold boiled beef, and telescopes,
And balls of string, and shrimps, and guns,
And chops, and tacks, and hats, and buns.

More of them

They brought him white kid gloves, and pails,
And candlesticks, and potted quails,
And capstan-bars, and scales and weights,
And ornaments for empty grates.

Why I mention these

My tale is not of these—oh no!
I only mention them to show

The divers gifts that divers men
Brought o'er the sea to BAILEY BEN.

His Confidant

A confidant had BAILEY B.,
A gay Mongolian dog was he;
I am not good at Turkish names,
And so I call him SIMPLE JAMES.

His Confidant's Countenance

A dreadful legend you might trace
In SIMPLE JAMES's honest face,
For there you read, in Nature's print,
"A Scoundrel of the Deepest Tint."

His Character

A deed of blood, or fire, or flames,
Was meat and drink to SIMPLE JAMES:
To hide his guilt he did not plan,
But owned himself a bad young man.

The Author to his Reader

And why on earth good BAILEY BEN
(The wisest, noblest, best of men)
Made SIMPLE JAMES his right-hand man
Is quite beyond my mental span.

The same, continued

But there—enough of gruesome deeds!
My heart, in thinking of them, bleeds;
And so let SIMPLE JAMES take wing,—
'Tis not of him I'm going to sing.

The Pasha's Clerk

Good PASHA BAILEY kept a clerk
(For BAILEY only made his mark),
His name was MATTHEW WYCOMBE COO,
A man of nearly forty-two.

His Accomplishments

No person that I ever knew
Could "yödel" half as well as Coo,
And Highlanders exclaimed, "Eh, weel!"
When Coo began to dance a reel.

His Kindness to the Pasha's Wives

He used to dance and sing and play
In such an unaffected way,
He cheered the unexciting lives
Of PASHA BAILEY's lovely wives.

The Author to his Reader

But why should I encumber you
With histories of MATTHEW COO?

Let MATTHEW Coo at once take wing,—
'Tis not of Coo I'm going to sing.

The Author's Muse

Let me recall my wandering Muse;
She *shall* be steady if I choose—
She roves, instead of helping me
To tell the deeds of BAILEY B.

The Pasha's Visitor

One morning knocked, at half-past eight,
A tall Red Indian at his gate.
In Turkey, as you're p'raps aware,
Red Indians are extremely rare.

The Visitor's Outfit

Moccasins decked his graceful legs,
His eyes were black, and round as eggs,
And on his neck, instead of beads,
Hung several Catawampous seeds.

What the Visitor said

"Ho, ho!" he said, "thou pale-faced one,
Poor offspring of an Eastern sun,
You've *never* seen the Red Man skip
Upon the banks of the Mississipp!"

The Author's Moderation

To say that BAILEY oped his eyes
Would feebly paint his great surprise—
To say it almost made him die
Would be to paint it much too high.

The Author to his Reader

But why should I ransack my head
To tell you all that Indian said;
We'll let the Indian man take wing,—
'Tis not of him I'm going to sing.

The Reader to the Author

Come, come, I say, that's quite enough
Of this absurd disjointed stuff;
Now let's get on to that affair
About LIEUTENANT-COLONEL FLARE.

W. S. Gilbert

PATIENCE

When ski-ing in the Engadine
My hat blew off down a ravine.
My son, who went to fetch it back,
Slipped through an icy glacier's crack
And then got permanently stuck.
It really was infernal luck:
My hat was practically new—
I loved my little Henry too—
And I may have to wait for years
Till either of them reappears.

Harry Graham

From *PENCIL STUBS*

To a Reviewer Who Admired My Book

Few men in any age have second sight.
But never doubt *your* gift. You are right! You are right!

After a Fire

Some of my books were burned. I must
believe at last there is a holy dust.

John Ciardi

From *PERAMBULATOR POEMS*

When I was christened
they held me up
and poured some water
out of a cup.

The trouble was
it fell on me,
and I and water
don't agree.

A lot of christeners
stood and listened:
I let them know
that I was christened.

David McCord

THE PERFECT REACTIONARY

As I was sitting in my chair
I knew the bottom wasn't there,
Nor legs nor back, but *I just sat,*
Ignoring little things like that.

Hughes Mearns

PLAIN TALK FOR A PACHYDERM

Spruce up, O Baggy Elephant!
Firm and conform that globular figger,
For, although you yourself may think you've outgrown your
    britches,
Either you've lost weight or your coveralls have stretched:
They appear to be a whole mountain size bigger.

Now, this isn't Skid Row on the Bowery, you know!
You could use a lot more starch in your clothes,
Iron you maybe a billion wrinkles before the next opening of
    the gates,
And tuck up that dangling nose
Which snuffles around your ankles like an old loose stocking
    that got lost from a foot.

You never can tell just who might show up out here, you
    know,
You sloppy pachyderm!
You don't want people whispering amongst themselves,
"Hey, get a load of this big bum!"

Peggy Bennett

THE PLATYPUS

My child, the Duck-billed Platypus
A sad example sets for us:
From him we learn how Indecision
Of character provokes Derision.
This vacillating Thing, you see,
Could not decide which he would be,
Fish, Flesh or Fowl, and chose all three.
The scientists were sorely vexed
To classify him; so perplexed
Their brains, that they, with Rage at bay,
Called him a horrid name one day,—
A name that baffles, frights and shocks us,
Ornithorhynchus Paradoxus.

Oliver Herford

From *POEMS IN PRAISE OF PRACTICALLY NOTHING*

You buy some flowers for your table;
You tend them tenderly as you're able;
You fetch them water from hither and thither—
What thanks do you get for it all? They wither.

*

You take a bath and sit there bathing
In water cold, in water scathing;
You scrub till you're sans an epidermis
And feel like a regular bathing Hermes.
You do not waste a single minute;
The tub shows you worked while in it;
You dry, and do some honest rooting
For such remarkable abluting.
Well, a day goes by, or ten, or thirty,
And what thanks do you get? You're just as dirty!

*

You leap out of bed; you start to get ready;
You dress and you dress till you feel unsteady;
Hours go by, and you're still busy
Putting on clothes, till your brain is dizzy.
Do you flinch, do you quit, do you go out naked?
The least little button, you don't forsake it.
What thanks do you get? Well, for all this mess, yet
When night comes around you've got to undress yet.

Samuel Hoffenstein

THE PRATER

Lysander talks extremely well:
On any subject let him dwell,
     His tropes and figures will content Ye:
He should possess to all degrees
The art of talk, he practises
     Full fourteen hours in four and twenty.

Matthew Prior

THE PRAYER OF CYRUS BROWN

"The proper way for a man to pray,"
    Said Deacon Lemuel Keyes,
"And the only proper attitude
    Is down upon his knees."

"No, I should say the way to pray,"
    Said Rev. Doctor Wise,
"Is standing straight with outstretched arms
    And rapt and upturned eyes."

"Oh, no; no, no," said Elder Slow,
    "Such posture is too proud:
A man should pray with eyes fast closed
    And head contritely bowed."

"It seems to me his hands should be
    Austerely clasped in front,
With both thumbs pointing toward the ground,"
    Said Rev. Doctor Blunt.

"Las' year I fell in Hodgkin's well
    Head first," said Cyrus Brown,
"With both my heels a-stickin' up,
    My head a-pinting down;

"An' I made a prayer right then an' there—
    Best prayer I ever said,
The prayingest prayer I ever prayed
    A-standing on my head."

Sam Walter Foss

PRESENCE OF MIND

When, with my little daughter Blanche,
    I climbed the Alps, last summer,
I saw a dreadful avalanche
    About to overcome her;
And, as it swept her down the slope,
    I vaguely wondered whether
I should be wise to cut the rope
    That held us twain together.

   *   *   *   *

I must confess I'm glad I did,
But still I miss the child—poor kid!

Harry Graham

PRIG: EPITAPH

Here lies a man who always thought
That he was acting as he ought.
He turned his cheek to every blow
And never said 'I told you so',
Nor claimed with any outward spite
The mean revenge of being right.
He died at three score years and ten
Detested by his fellow men
But conscious of a Heavenly Crown—

*   *   *   *

'Go *down!*' St. Peter said, 'GO DOWN!'

Colin Ellis

THE PURIST

I give you now Professor Twist,
A conscientious scientist.
Trustees exclaimed, "He never bungles!"
And sent him off to distant jungles.
Camped on a tropic riverside,
One day he missed his loving bride.
She had, the guide informed him later,
Been eaten by an alligator.
Professor Twist could not but smile.
"You mean," he said, "a crocodile."

Ogden Nash

THE RAIN IT RAINETH

The rain it raineth on the just
    And also on the unjust fella;
But chiefly on the just, because
    The unjust steals the just's umbrella.

Lord Bowen

rain or hail
sam done
the best he kin
till they digged his hole

:sam was a man

stout as a bridge
rugged as a bear
slickern a weazel
how be you

(sun or snow)

gone into what
like all them kings
you read about
and on him sings

a whippoorwill;

heart was big
as the world aint square
with room for the devil
and his angels too

yes,sir

what may be better
or what may be worse
and what may be clover
clover clover

(nobody'll know)

sam was a man
grinned his grin
done his chores
laid him down.

Sleep well

    e. e. cummings

THE REMEDY WORSE THAN
THE DISEASE

I sent for Ratcliffe; was so ill,
    That other doctors gave me over:
He felt my pulse, prescribed his pill,
    And I was likely to recover.

But when the wit began to wheeze,
    And wine had warm'd the politician,
Cured yesterday of my disease,
    I died last night of my physician.

                 Matthew Prior

ROAST SWAN SONG

From *Carmina Burana*

Aforetime, by the waters wan,
This lovely body I put on:
In life I was a stately swan.

Ah me! Ah me!
Now browned and basted thoroughly.

The cook now turns me round and turns me.
The hurrying waiter next concerns me,
But oh, this fire, how fierce it burns me!

Ah me! Ah me!

Would I might glide, my plumage fluffing,
On pools to feel the cool wind soughing,
Rather than burst with pepper-stuffing.

Ah me! Ah me!

Once I was whiter than the snow,
The fairest bird that earth could show;
Now I am blacker than the crow.

Ah me! Ah me!

Here I am dished upon the platter.
I cannot fly. Oh, what's the matter?
Lights flash, teeth clash—I fear the latter.

Ouch! . . . Ouch! . . .

The Goliard Poets
Translated by George F. Whicher

THE SEA

Behold the wonders of the mighty deep,
Where crabs and lobsters learn to creep,
And little fishes learn to swim,
And clumsy sailors tumble in.

Anonymous

SIGNS OF THE ZODIAC

(Symmetrics)

I. ARIES : RAM

Rambunctious Ram, still sporting down the glade,
Hellê fell off his back and drowned. Fair
         maid   made
Hellespont. His Golden Fleece no sham,
Safe on a sacrifice is all-star Ram.

II. TAURUS : BULL

Taurus, whose reddening eye Aldebaran
Looked last upon Europa, looks at
         man : man
Hangs round Zenith's door. What nymphal chorus
Of Hyads, Pleiads in floorless floorshow, Taurus!

III. GEMINI : TWINS

Castor to Pollux: "Heracles, Apollo . . . .
The Greeks have twinned us twice! Advice to
         follow?" "Follow
To Egypt where we're kids. In vaster
Skies of Araby, peacocks. Over. Castor."

IV. CANCER : CRAB

Out of this world, your second name is fun,
Crab! *Crab!* Sidereal sidewise solstice
                one : one
Likes your pale vermicular redoubt,
The Beehive, with celestial bees about.

V. LEO : LION

Leo the Lion roars. At whom? Such fuss
Was not *your* way to stardom,
              Regulus : Regulus—
Cosmic address, Leo's P.O.,
"Well, I'm in charge of Leonids, not Leo."

VI. VIRGO : VIRGIN

Virgo, below the Dipper, spike of grain
In hand, the sinning world can see you
                plain : plain
Living and the highest thinking! Ergo,
Who knows *what* Hesiod thought about you, Virgo?

VII. LIBRA : BALANCE

Balance of two syndetic days and nights
Transcending budget, arms, and civil
              rights   rights
Human wrongs no more than man's poor talents.
You find us wanting, Libra—wanting balance.

VIII. Scorpio : Scorpion

Myth makes Orion say that he would kill
All animals on earth. He reckoned
                    ill : ill-
Starred when Scorpio stung him. Now he's with
His Killer high up attic. End of myth.

IX. Sagittarius : Archer

Archer with bended bow, we know your lot:
Ixion's scions—centaurs, were you
                    not? Not
Privy to his exit, man's departure
May be one supersonic arrow, Archer!

X. Capricornus : Goat

If Latin *caper* (goat) and *cornu* (horn)
Be syllables to please the noble
                    born : borne
In upon us, one malodorous whiff,
Half goat, half fish, all you—then where's that *if?*

XI. Aquarius : Water Bearer

Aquarius, the Water Bearer, bears
The vintage liquid of the world. Who
                    shares   shares
Life itself, since life however various
Depends on water. Any wine, Aquarius?

XII. Pisces : Fishes

Fish. Silvery in themselves. The silver night
Reveals a pair, tails tied, in sorry
                    plight : "Plight
Thee my troth," said Eros. "As you wish."
Who said that? Aphroditê? The poor, poor fish!

David McCord

SOME NATURAL HISTORY

the patagonian
penguin
is a most
peculiar
bird
he lives on
pussy
willows
and his tongue
is always furred
the porcupine
of chile
sleeps his life away
and that is how
the needles
get into the hay
the argentinian
oyster
is a very
subtle gink
for when he s
being eaten
he pretends he is
a skink
when you see
a sea gull
sitting
on a bald man s dome
she likely thinks
she s nesting

on her rocky
island home
do not tease
the inmates
when strolling
through the zoo
for they have
their finer feelings
the same
as me and you
oh deride not
the camel
if grief should
make him die
his ghost will come
to haunt you
with tears
in either eye
and the spirit of
a camel
in the midnight gloom
can be so very
cheerless
as it wanders
round the room

Don Marquis

SOMEBODY SAID THAT IT COULDN'T BE DONE

Somebody said that it couldn't be done—
But he, with a grin, replied
He'd never be one to say it couldn't be done—
Leastways, not 'til he'd tried.
So he buckled right in, with a trace of a grin;
By golly, he went right to it.
He tackled The Thing That Couldn't Be Done!
And he couldn't do it.

Anonymous

THE SORROWS OF WERTHER

Werther had a love for Charlotte
    Such as words could never utter;
Would you know how first he met her?
    She was cutting bread and butter.

Charlotte was a married lady,
    And a moral man was Werther,
And for all the wealth of Indies,
    Would do nothing for to hurt her.

So he sigh'd and pined and ogled,
    And his passion boil'd and bubbled,
Till he blew his silly brains out,
    And no more was by it troubled.

Charlotte, having seen his body
    Borne before her on a shutter,
Like a well-conducted person,
    Went on cutting bread and butter.

    William Makepeace Thackeray

Note: Die Leiden des Jungen Werthers (The Sorrow of Young Werther), by the German Johann Wolfgang von Goethe, is the story of Goethe's own love affair with one Charlotte Buff. Its sentimental excesses undoubtedly appealed to Thackeray's delicious sense of humor!

From *SPEAKING OF TELEVISION*

Robin Hood

Zounds, gramercy, and rootity-toot!
Here comes the man in the green flannel suit.

Reflections Dental

How pure, how beautiful, how fine
Do teeth on television shine!
No flutist flutes, no dancer twirls,
But comes equipped with matching pearls.
Gleeful announcers all are born
With sets like rows of hybrid corn.
Clowns, critics, clergy, commentators,
Ventriloquists and roller skaters,
M.C.s who beat their palms together,
The girl who diagrams the weather,
The crooner crooning for his supper—
All flash white treasures, lower and upper.
With miles of smiles the airwaves teem,
And each an orthodontist's dream.

'Twould please my eye as gold a miser's—
One charmer with uncapped incisors.

The Importance of Being Western

Wyatt Earp
Rides tall in the stearp.

Phyllis McGinley

THE SYCOPHANTIC FOX AND
THE GULLIBLE RAVEN

A raven sat upon a tree,
   And not a word he spoke, for
His beak contained a piece of Brie,
   Or, maybe, it was Roquefort?
      We'll make it any kind you please—
      At all events, it was a cheese.

Beneath the tree's umbrageous limb
   A hungry fox sat smiling;
He saw the raven watching him,
   And spoke in words beguiling:
      "J'admire," said he, "ton beau plumage."
      (The which was simply persiflage.)

Two things there are, no doubt you know,
   To which a fox is used—
A rooster that is bound to crow,
   A crow that's bound to roost,
      And whichsoever he espies
      He tells the most unblushing lies.

"Sweet fowl," he said, "I understand
   You're more than merely natty:
I hear you sing to beat the band
   And Adelina Patti.
      Pray render with your liquid tongue
      A bit from Götterdämmerung."

This subtle speech was aimed to please
    The crow, and it succeeded:
He thought no bird in all the trees
    Could sing as well as he did.
        In flattery completely doused
        He gave the "Jewel Song" from *Faust*.

But gravitation's law, of course,
    As Isaac Newton showed it,
Exerted on the cheese its force,
    And elsewhere soon bestowed it.
        In fact, there is no need to tell
        What happened when to earth it fell.

I blush to add that when the bird
    Took in the situation,
He said one brief, emphatic word,
    Unfit for publication.
        The fox was greatly startled, but
        He only sighed and answered "Tut!"

THE MORAL is: A fox is bound
    To be a shameless sinner.
And also: When the cheese comes round
    You know it's after dinner.
        But (what is only known to few)
        The fox is after dinner, too.

                Guy Wetmore Carryl

TARTUFFE, Act I, Scene 4

ORGON, CLÉANTE, DORINE

ORGON

Ah, Brother, good-day.

CLÉANTE

Well, welcome back. I'm sorry I can't stay.
How was the country? Blooming, I trust, and green?

ORGON

Excuse me, Brother; just one moment.
(*To Dorine:*)

Dorine . . .

(*To Cléante:*)
To put my mind at rest, I always learn
The household news the moment I return.
(*To Dorine:*)
Has all been well, these two days I've been gone?
How are the family? What's been going on?

DORINE

Your wife, two days ago, had a bad fever,
And a fierce headache which refused to leave her.

ORGON

Ah. And Tartuffe?

DORINE

Tartuffe? Why, he's round and red,
Bursting with health, and excellently fed.

ORGON
Poor fellow!

DORINE
                 That night, the mistress was unable
To take a single bite at the dinner-table.
Her headache-pains, she said, were simply hellish.

ORGON
Ah. And Tartuffe?

DORINE
                    He ate his meal with relish,
And zealously devoured in her presence
A leg of mutton and a brace of pheasants.

ORGON
Poor fellow!

DORINE
               Well, the pains continued strong,
And so she tossed and tossed the whole night long,
Now icy-cold, now burning like a flame.
We sat beside her bed till morning came.

ORGON
Ah. And Tartuffe?

DORINE
                  Why, having eaten, he rose
And sought his room, already in a doze,
Got into his warm bed, and snored away
In perfect peace until the break of day.

ORGON

Poor fellow!

DORINE

         After much ado, we talked her
Into dispatching someone for the doctor.
He bled her, and the fever quickly fell.

ORGON

Ah. And Tartuffe?

DORINE

          He bore it very well.
To keep his cheerfulness at any cost,
And make up for the blood *Madame* had lost,
He drank, at lunch, four beakers full of port.

ORGON

Poor fellow!

DORINE

        Both are doing well, in short.
I'll go and tell *Madame* that you've expressed
Keen sympathy and anxious interest.

Molière
Translated by Richard Wilbur

THEORY

Into love and out again,
    Thus I went, and thus I go.
Spare your voice, and hold your pen—
    Well and bitterly I know
All the songs were ever sung,
    All the words were ever said;
Could it be, when I was young,
    Some one dropped me on my head?

Dorothy Parker

There is Hallelujah Hannah
    Walking backwards down the lane,
And I hear the loud Hosanna
    Of regenerated Jane;
And Lieutenant Isabella
    In the centre of them comes,
Dealing blows with her umbrella
    On the trumpets and the drums.

A. E. Housman

Note: "Perhaps I may myself write a Hymn-Book for use in the
Salvation Army," A. E. Housman wrote in a letter. See also
" 'Hallelujah' was the only observation."

There was a faith-healer of Deal
Who said, "Although pain isn't real,
    If I sit on a pin
    And I puncture my skin,
I dislike what I *fancy* I feel!"

Anonymous

There was a young woman named Bright,
Whose speed was much faster than light.
    She set out one day
    In a relative way,
And returned on the previous night.

Anonymous

'TIS MIDNIGHT

'Tis midnight, and the setting sun
    Is slowly rising in the west;
The rapid rivers slowly run,
    The frog is on his downy nest.
The pensive goat and sportive cow,
Hilarious, leap from bough to bough.

Unknown

'TIS SWEET TO ROAM

'Tis sweet to roam when morning's light
    Resounds across the deep;
And the crystal song of the woodbine bright
    Hushes the rocks to sleep,
And the blood-red moon in the blaze of noon
    Is bathed in a crumbling dew,
And the wolf rings out with a glittering shout,
    To-whit, to-whit, to-whoo!

Unknown

TO A FRIEND: CONSTRUCTIVE
CRITICISM

Lift sunward yr considerable nose,
    fling wide th' abyss of yr mouth,
And you'll make a presentable sun-dial for all who pass by.

The Emperor Trajan
Translated by Dudley Fitts

TO A LADY IN A PHONE BOOTH

Plump occupant of Number Eight,
    Outside whose door I shift my parcels
And wait and wait and wait and wait
    With aching nerves and metatarsals,
I long to comprehend the truth:
What keeps you sitting in that booth?

What compact holds you like a stone?
    Whose voice, whose summons rich with power,
Has fixed you to the telephone
    These past three-quarters of an hour?
Can this be love? Or thorns or prickles?
And where do you get all those nickels?

Say, was the roof above you sold
    By nameless landlord, cruel and craven,
Till, driven by imperious cold,
    You find this nook your only haven?
Yield me the instrument you hoard,
And I will share my bed and board.

Perhaps you choose such public place
    To do your lips and change your vesture.
You have not swooned, in any case.
    A motion, an occasional gesture,
Assures me you are safe inside.
You do not sleep. You have not died.

That paper clutched within your fist—
    I cannot quite make out the heading—
Madam, is that a formal list?
    Do you, by chance, arrange a wedding?
Or—dreadful thought I dare not speak!—
Perhaps you rent here by the week.

Well, likely I shall never know.
    My arches fall, my patience ravels.
And with these bundles I must go,
    Frustrated, forth upon my travels.
Behind the unrevealing pane
The mystery and you remain.

Yet, as I totter out of line,
    A faint suspicion waxes stronger.
Oh, could it be your feet, like mine,
    Would simply bear you up no longer?
So did you happen, unaware,
Upon this cubicle, with chair,

And did it seem in all the town
One spot where you could just sit down?

Phyllis McGinley

TO A SLOW WALKER AND QUICK EATER

So slowly you walk, and so quickly you eat,
You should march with your mouth, and devour with
  your feet.

Gotthold Ephraim Lessing

TO MY EMPTY PURSE

To you, my purse, and to none other wight,
Complain I, for ye be my lady dere;
I am sorry now that ye be light,
For, certes, ye now make me heavy chere;
Me were as lefe be laid upon a bere,
For which unto your mercy thus I crie,
Be heavy againe, or els mote I die.

Now vouchsafe this day or it be night,
That I of you the blissful sowne may here,
Or see your color like the sunne bright,
That of yellowness had never pere;
Ye are my life, ye be my hertes sterc,
Queen of comfort and of good companie,
Be heavy againe, or els mote I die.

Now purse, thou art to me my lives light,
And saviour, as downe in this world here,
Out of this towne helpe me by your might,
Sith that you will not be my treasure,
For I am slave as nere as any frere,
But I pray unto your curtesie,
Be heavy againe, or els mote I die.

Geoffrey Chaucer

TO PHOEBE

"Gentle, modest, little flower,
　　Sweet epitome of May,
Love me but for half-an-hour,
　　Love me, love me, little fay."
Sentences so fiercely flaming
　　In your tiny shell-like ear,
I should always be exclaiming
　　If I loved you, PHOEBE, dear.

"Smiles that thrill from any distance
　　Shed upon me while I sing!
Please ecstaticise existence,
　　Love me, oh thou fairy thing!"
Words like these, outpouring sadly,
　　You'd perpetually hear,
If I loved you, fondly, madly;—
　　But I do not, PHOEBE, dear.

W. S. Gilbert

TO THE TERRESTIAL GLOBE

BY A MISERABLE WRETCH

Roll on, thou ball, roll on!
Through pathless realms of Space
    Roll on!
What though I'm in a sorry case?
What though I cannot meet my bills?
What though I suffer toothache's ills?
What though I swallow countless pills?
  Never *you* mind!
    Roll on!

Roll on, thou ball, roll on!
Through seas of inky air
    Roll on!
It's true I have no shirts to wear;
It's true my butcher's bill is due;
It's true my prospects all look blue—
But don't let that unsettle you:
  Never *you* mind!
    Roll on!

        [It rolls on.

       W. S. Gilbert

A TONVERSATION WITH BABY

"Was it a little baby
   With wide, unwinking eyes,
Propped in his baby carriage,
   Looking so wise?

"Oh, what a pwitty baby!
   Oh, what a sweety love!
Who is oo thinkin', baby,
   And dweamin' of?

"Is oo wond'rin' 'bout de doggie
   A-fwiskin' here 'n dere?
Is oo watchin' de baby birdies
   Everywhere?

" 'N all de funny peoples
   'N a funny sings oo sees?
What is oo sinkin' of, baby?
   Tell me, please.

" 'Z oo sinkin' of tisses, tunnin,
   'N wannin 'n wannin for some?
O tweety goo swummy doddle,
   O yummy yum!"

Then spoke that solemn baby,
   Wise as a little gnome:
"You get in the baby carriage;
   I'll push you home."

Morris Bishop

TOURIST TIME

This fat woman in canvas knickers
Gapes seriously at everything.
We might be a city of the dead
Or cave men
Instead of simple town folk.
We have nothing to show
That can't be seen better somewhere else,
Yet for this woman the wonder ceases not.

Madam, the most extraordinary thing in this town
Is the shape of your legs.

O communication!
O rapid transit!

F. R. Scott

A TRAGIC STORY

There lived a sage in days of yore,
And he a handsome pigtail wore;
But wondered much and sorrowed more,
　　Because it hung behind him.

He mused upon this curious case,
And swore he'd change the pigtail's place,
And have it hanging at his face,
　　Not dangling there behind him.

Says he, "The mystery I've found—
I'll turn me round,"—he turned him round;
　　But still it hung behind him.

Then round and round, and out and in,
All day the puzzled sage did spin;
In vain—it mattered not a pin—
　　The pigtail hung behind him.

And right and left, and round about,
And up and down, and in and out,
He turned; but still the pigtail stout
　　Hung steadily behind him.

And though his efforts never slack,
And though he twist and twirl and tack,
Alas! still faithful to his back,
　　The pigtail hangs behind him.

　　　　William Makepeace Thackeray

TRAVELLER'S CURSE
AFTER MISDIRECTION

(From the Welsh)

May they wander stage by stage
Of the same vain pilgrimage,
Stumbling on, age after age,
Night and day, mile after mile,
At each and every step, a stile;
At each and every stile, withal,
May they catch their feet and fall;
At each and every fall they take,
May a bone within them break,
And may the bones that break within
Not be, for variation's sake,
Now rib, now thigh, now arm, now shin,
But always, without fail, THE NECK.

Robert Graves

TRIOLET AGAINST SISTERS

Sisters are always drying their hair.
    Locked into rooms, alone,
They pose at the mirror, shoulders bare,
Trying this way and that their hair,
Or fly importunate down the stair
    To answer a telephone.
Sisters are always drying their hair,
    Locked into rooms, alone.

Phyllis McGinley

TWELVE ARTICLES

I

Lest it may more quarrels breed,
I will never hear you read.

II

By disputing, I will never
To convince you once endeavor.

III

When a paradox you stick to,
I will never contradict you.

IV

When I talk and you are heedless,
I will show no anger needless.

V

When your speeches are absurd,
I will ne'er object a word.

VI

When you furious argue wrong,
I will grieve and hold my tongue.

VII

Not a jest or humorous story
Will I ever tell before ye:
To be chidden for explaining,
When you quite mistake the meaning.

VIII

Never more will I suppose,
You can taste my verse or prose.

IX

You no more at me shall fret,
While I teach and you forget.

X

You shall never hear me thunder,
When you blunder on, and blunder.

XI

Show your poverty of spirit,
And in dress place all your merit;
Give yourself ten thousand airs:
That with me shall break no squares.

XII

Never will I give advice,
Till you please to ask me thrice:
Which if you in scorn reject,
'T will be just as I expect.

Thus we both shall have our ends
And continue special friends.

Jonathan Swift

TWO MEN

There be two men of all mankind
   That I should like to know about;
But search and question where I will,
   I cannot ever find them out.

Melchizedek, he praised the Lord,
   And gave some wine to Abraham;
But who can tell what else he did
   Must be more learned than I am.

Ucalegon, he lost his house
   When Agamemnon came to Troy;
But who can tell me who he was—
   I'll pray the gods to give him joy.

There be two men of all mankind
   That I'm forever thinking on:
They chase me everywhere I go,—
   Melchizedek, Ucalegon.

Edwin Arlington Robinson

UNEARNED INCREMENT

The Old Mandarin
Always perplexes his friend the Adjuster
At the Prune Exchange Bank
By adding his balances together
In the Chinese fashion.
For example: he once had $5000 in the bank
And drew various checks against it.
He drew $2000; thus leaving a balance of $3000.
He drew $1500; thus leaving a balance of $1500.
He drew $900; thus leaving a balance of $600.
He drew $600; thus leaving a balance of   000.
       $5000 $5100
Yet, as you see, when he adds his various balances
He finds that they total $5100
And the Old Mandarin therefore maintains
There should still be $100 to his credit.
They had to engage the Governor of the Federal Reserve
To explain the fallacy to him.

Christopher Morley

A VALENTINE FOR A LADY

Darling, at the Beautician's you buy
Your (a) hair
     (b) complexion
     (c) lips
     (d) dimples, &
     (e) teeth.

For a like amount you could just as well buy a face.

Lucilius
Translated by Dudley Fitts

WHAT THE MOON SAW

Two statesmen met by moonlight.
Their ease was partly feigned.
They glanced about the prairie.
Their faces were constrained.
In various ways aforetime
They had misled the state,
Yet did it so politely
Their henchmen thought them great.
They sat beneath a hedge and spake
No word, but had a smoke.
A satchel passed from hand to hand.
Next day, the deadlock broke.

Vachel Lindsay

WHAT'S MY THOUGHT LIKE?

Quest.—Why is a Pump like Viscount Castlereagh?
  Answ.—Because it is like a slender thing of wood,
That up and down its awkward arm doth sway,
And cooly spout, and spout, and spout away,
  In one weak, washy, everlasting flood!

Thomas Moore

William Penn
Was the most level-headed of men;
He only had one mania—
Pennsylvania.

William Jay Smith

THE WISHES OF AN ELDERLY MAN

(Wished at a Garden Party, June 1914)

I wish I loved the Human Race;
I wish I loved its silly face;
I wish I liked the way it walks;
I wish I liked the way it talks;
And when I'm introduced to one
I wish I thought *What Jolly Fun!*

Sir Walter Raleigh

WRATH

Higgledy-piggledy
Ludwig van Beethoven
Scornful of cheer, and of
Hearing forlorn,

Spitefully hissing, sat
Writing unplayable
Pianississississimo
Notes for the horn.

John Hollander

YOUR LITTLE HANDS

Your little hands,
Your little feet,
Your little mouth—
Oh, God, how sweet!

Your little nose,
Your little ears,
Your eyes, that shed
Such little tears!

Your little voice,
So soft and kind;
Your little soul,
Your little mind!

Samuel Hoffenstein

INDEX OF TITLES

INDEX OF FIRST LINES

INDEX OF AUTHORS

INDEX OF TRANSLATORS